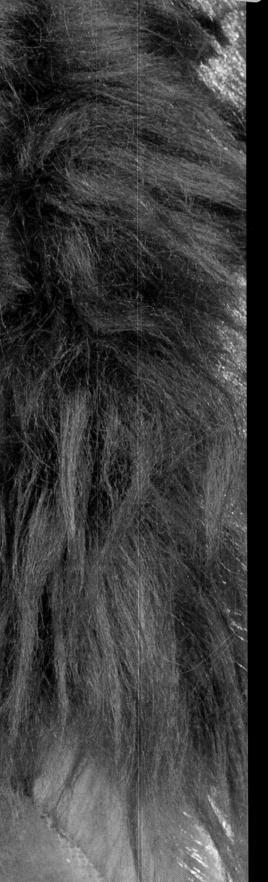

Contents

Introduction

Pale pink base

FACE PAINTING has become more and more popular in recent years and with the kind of water-based face paint now available, it's possible for anyone to achieve really startling designs with just a little practice. Out of all the faces we've been asked to create, animals are the most popular. In this book, therefore, we've provided plenty of animal faces for you to copy and adapt. If you're new to face painting, look at the step by step photos on the right which give you the basic techniques of using face paints.

Glitter gel is a fun extra.

1 Always apply the base coat first with a sponge. Keep your sponge fairly dry. If you make it too wet, the paint may become streaky. Take the paint up to the hairline and just under the chin.

Materials

The best paints to buy are water-based face paints. These are quick and easy to put on. They also dry fast and won't smudge (as long as they don't get wet), and they're easy to wash off with a little soap and water. You can buy paints in single pots, or in palettes which contain several colours and a brush and sponge. If you're going to do a lot of face painting, it's worth buying several brushes of different thicknesses and a selection of sponges. Look out for stipple sponges which are good for creating texture.

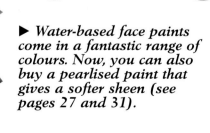

▶ *Water-based face paints come in a fantastic range of colours. Now, you can also buy a pearlised paint that gives a softer sheen (see pages 27 and 31).*

Paint over the lips, too.

Apply brushstrokes with a firm, steady hand. Try not to sketch.

Apply glitter gel with a dry brush.

2 Apply one colour at a time. When painting a large patch of colour – like this beak – draw the outline first with a fine brush, then fill it in with a thicker one.

3 Add paler colours before darker ones. Here, we've overlapped the colours slightly and used shorter brushstrokes to give the appearance of feathers.

4 Darker colours are usually added last. Here, we've outlined the beak, painted lines on the nose and lips and added the feathery design between the eyes – all in black.

Basics

1 Before you begin, make sure that you have one or two pots of clean water handy. Remember to change the water frequently and keep all your brushes and sponges scrupulously clean.

2 Always apply water-based make-up to clean, dry skin.

3 Never use face paints on someone with a skin problem. If you're not sure, test a small patch of paint on your model's wrist before you begin.

4 Try to keep your designs simple and quick. Young children find it hard to sit still for much more than five minutes!

5 Sit your models on a high stool or chair. Keep them steady by resting one hand on their head.

6 Always take care when painting around the eyes. When painting the top eyelids, ask your models to keep their eyes closed until the paint has dried. Never paint too close to the bottom of the eyes.

▶ *Cats and tigers are perhaps the most popular animal faces of all. See pages 9 and 12-15 for inspiration.*

Pet Pals

ALL CHILDREN, especially younger ones, love having their faces painted as puppies, kittens, mice or rabbits. These are all easy designs to start with when you are new to face painting. They're also useful for more experienced face painters working at fund-raising events or parties with many faces to paint in a short amount of time. On very small children, keep your designs really simple. You don't even need a base coat – just paint a little nose and whiskers for a kitten and some black and white spots for a spotty dog.

Dizzy Dog

1 Apply a thin light brown base over the whole face with a fairly dry sponge.

2 Using a thick brush, paint in the large white patches over the eyes and the area around the nose and lower cheeks.

3 Outline the white eye patches in chestnut brown.

4 Paint the nose and upper lip in black. Outline the white area around the mouth then, with a fine brush, add the feathery effect at the corner of the lips, the spots, and the black lines on the cheeks and at the corner of the eyes.

5 Finally, paint the lower lip in red or pink.

Tie long hair in bunches to look like shaggy ears.

Take paint up to the hairline.

Patch

1 Sponge a white base all over the face, keeping the sponge fairly dry.

2 Add the black patches (taking care not to paint too close to the eye), the feathery eyebrow, the nose and the mouth.

3 Paint in the red tongue.

A baseball cap turned to one side works well with this character.

Pink Rabbit

1 Apply a thin white base with a sponge. Using the same sponge, blend some light pink over the cheeks.

2 Paint in the two pink triangular patches above the eyes with a brush.

3 Paint in the area around the mouth and the teeth in white.

4 With a fine brush, add the black lines on the forehead, cheeks and below the eyes. Outline the teeth, then add the spots above the lips and paint in the round nose.

5 Finally, paint the lips pink.

Add dots and lines on the cheeks for whiskers.

THE TWO MICE FACES below show how you can achieve quite different effects by simply changing your base colours and adapting the features slightly. The tawny cat face looks difficult at first glance but uses only four colours. The dramatic effect is achieved by using bold overlapping brushstrokes.

Cheeky Mouse

1 Use a sponge to apply a thin grey base coat. Use the same sponge to blend some pink over the cheeks.

2 Paint in the the white eyes and add the dots over the mouth with a fine brush.

3 Add the pink nose.

4 With a brush, outline the eyes, fill in the upper lip and add the black lines.

5 Paint the lower lip in red.

Party Mouse

1 Apply turquoise around the edges of the face with a barely damp sponge. Using the same sponge, blend in pink over the cheeks and on the chin.

2 Paint in the eyes and the area around the mouth in pale pink.

3 Add the white teeth.

4 Add the outlines, nose and whiskers in black.

5 Add the white highlights with a very fine brush.

Tawny Cat

1 Sponge a beige or a light pink base over the whole face.

2 With a brush, paint in pink above and below the eyes and down the length and on the tip of the nose.

3 Paint tawny patches above the eyes and brush two lines down the sides of the nose.

4 Paint in the white muzzle then all the black outlines with a fine brush, adding lines around the eyes and down the nose.

5 With a wide, flat brush, add the white, black and brown dashes, one colour at a time, to create the appearance of fur.

Brush on the paint in the direction that the fur would grow. —————

Add a touch of glitter above the eyes and around the nose.

Black cardboard ears attached to an elastic headband.

Farmyard Friends

SIMPLY PAINTING a whole animal on a cheek, hand or arm, is quick and fun to do. Look out for other farmyard animal motifs you could copy, such as a munching cow or a mother hen with her yellow chicks. For a dramatic full face, try painting this white feathery duck.

Fluffy Duck

1 Using a sponge, apply a white base over the whole face.

2 Paint in the blue patches above the eyes with a brush.

3 Paint in the wide yellow beak.

4 Add the black lines around the eyes, nostrils and beak.

5 Paint the lower lip in dark blue, extending the natural line of the mouth.

6 Finish off with the feather design. Paint in the pale blue V-shapes first, then add the orange, then the dark blue.

Cockerel

Paint in the red and green base colours, add white and yellow highlights, then outline in black. Add the bird's red crest and brown feet with a fine brush and dot in its eye.

Pink Pig

As with the lamb, add the base colour first – here a pale pink. Add darker pink under the pig's belly then outline in brown. Finish off with some green tufts of grass around its feet.

Leaping Lamb

Paint the woolly white coat, add the black legs, tail and head, then paint black swirls over the coat with a fine brush.

A white feathery boa makes a perfect headdress.

Always keep paint away from the eyes.

Wild Cat

1 Sponge beige paint over the centre of the face.

2 Using the same sponge, add white over the nose and mouth and then chestnut or rusty-coloured paint over the rest of the face.

3 With a thick brush, paint in the dark brown lines over the eyes. Then, with a finer brush, add the two lines down the sides of the nose.

4 Paint the cat's top teeth on the model's lower lip and the bottom teeth on the chin.

5 Paint the rest of the mouth shape in black, then add the black nose and spots.

6 Add red around the eyes and paint in the whiskers.

Colourful Cats

CATS CAN BE REALISTIC like our fierce wild cat, or much more fanciful like the fantasy cats below. Even though they look very different, each of these cats has a dark nose, boldly painted whiskers, and distinctive curved lines or patches over the eyes. We've given a mottled texture to the wild cat by applying yellow paint with a stipple sponge. On the fantasy cats, we've used a touch of glitter.

Pink Cat

There are no rules about which base colours to use on a fantasy cat but do choose different colour combinations with care. Here, the bright pink and purple work well together, especially with white.

Sponge paint into the hair.

Add silver glitter with a fine brush.

Add gold glitter on the forehead and chin for extra sparkle.

Curved lines should be painted in one bold, continuous brushstroke.

Blue Cat

To paint this cat, first apply a blue base then sponge yellow over the forehead, down the sides of the face and over the chin. Paint in the dark blue lines first, then add the white highlights. The lines around the outside of the face have been painted from the outside of the face towards the middle, and the colours have been blended slightly, to soften.

Paint curly whiskers and eyebrows wth a fine brush.

13

Big Cats

LIONS AND TIGERS have the same basic features as cats and kittens. Here, you can see that each face has a similar-shaped black nose, with a short black line running from just under the nose to the upper lip. The faces also have white muzzles and fan-shaped patches above the eyes. Colouring varies – the lion has a golden-yellow base and the tigers have distinctive orange and black markings. Fur patterns have been achieved in different ways – with fine feathery brushstrokes, bold lines or with a stippling effect.

Hands

Hands (and feet) can easily be painted to match your animal faces. Here, we've painted a stripy tiger hand in orange and black.

Golden Lion

1 Apply a yellow base over the whole face with a barely damp sponge then, with a clean sponge, dab white over the area around the mouth.

2 Using a brush, paint in the dark brown lines over the eyebrows then add the two finer lines curving from the eyes, out over the cheeks and back to the corners of the mouth.

3 Paint in white above the eyes and add the whiskers.

4 Paint the lower lip in red then add the black nose and spots.

5 Finish off with the feathery lines around the face, adding a little gold glitter for extra texture.

Keep your hand steady when you brush on the two brown lines.

Use the side of a wide flat brush to give the texture of short spiky fur.

Sponge paint into the hair or make a set of ears out of fur fabric.

Brush on stripes from the outside of the face towards the centre.

Sabre-Tooth Tiger

1 Sponge a yellow base over the whole face with a fairly dry sponge. Use the same sponge to blend orange paint around the outer edges of the face and white above the eyebrows.

2 Paint the muzzle and the sharp fangs in white.

3 Add the black nose, fill in the upper lip and paint the fine feathery outline around the muzzle and teeth.

4 Paint in the black fur using the side of a brush. Start with the area between the eyes, then do the cheeks. Use the same technique to apply white paint between the black brushstrokes.

5 Add a touch of yellow over the eyes.

6 Finish off with the red lines under the eyes and the drops of red on the teeth for blood.

Little Tiger

1 Apply a peachy coloured base coat, as near to the model's own natural colouring as possible.

2 Using a stipple sponge, dab some red paint over the cheeks and forehead.

3 Paint the rusty fan-shaped lines over the eyebrows.

4 Add the white lines above the eyes and around the mouth.

5 Paint in the black nose, mouth and whiskers.

6 Add the lines under the eyes and the bold black and brown stripes around the face.

15

Spots and Stripes

Giraffe

1 Sponge on a yellow base coat then paint in the beige patch around the mouth.

2 Paint in the brown eyes and nostrils and outline the mouth.

3 Add the black lines over the lips, extending the lines over each cheek.

4 Paint in the yellow squarish patches then outline in brown.

SOME ANIMALS have such distinctive markings on their coats that it is easy to make them into effective face-painting designs. Spotted leopards, stripy tigers and zebras, and giraffes with their yellow and brown patches, are particularly easy to adapt. Spots and stripes also make good body painting designs, as shown in the photograph below.

Paint in whole blocks of yellow before outlining in brown.

Body Painting

Body painting can be extremely dramatic. If you're doing it for a stage production, use bold patterns that will show up from a distance. Don't forget to cover every part of the body that will show, including underneath the arms, hands and feet.

Snow Leopard

1 Apply a white base coat over the whole face with a fairly dry sponge.

2 Paint in the white eye patches and the area around the mouth with a large brush.

3 Paint black over the eyelids and add the black outlines, nose and whiskers.

4 Using your finger, dab pink and black spots over the face, slightly overlapping each one. Add touches of silver glitter over the spots with a dry brush.

5 Finish off by painting the lower lip in pink.

Keep the whiskers very fine and slightly curved.

Zebra

1 Apply a white base then, with the same sponge, dab a little pink over the cheeks, forehead and chin.

2 Paint in the black circles around the eyes (keeping the paint away from the area just under the eyes), then the nose and mouth.

3 Brush on the black stripes.

17

Bear Hugs

Panda

To paint this panda, sponge on a white base then paint in the black design. The eye patches are round at the top but slope down over the cheeks to make the bear look a little sad and in need of a hug.

BEAR FACES can be easy and quick to do by simply sponging on a plain base coat then adding one or two extra colours with a thick brush – like the panda and teddies shown here – or they can take longer, like the brown bear with its painted fur. Paint a bear's nose and mouth in the same way as you would for a cat but without the whiskers. The main difference between a bear's and a cat's face is the eyes – for a bear, keep the patches around the eyes round rather than making them pointed or fan-shaped.

Teddies

1 Paint a light brown base over the whole face using a slightly damp sponge.

2 Paint large white circles around the eyes with a thick brush. Make the circles slightly thicker at the top than at the bottom.

3 With a brush, paint in the eyebrows, mouth, nose and dots in black.

▶ *These teddy faces are ideal for small children who find it hard to sit still for long.*

Brown Bear

1 Using a sponge and a little water, apply a light brown base over the whole face.

2 Paint in the round brown eye patches with a brush.

3 Using a fine brush, paint in the black nose and mouth. Add a thin line of black just under the upper lip and extend the line of the mouth.

4 Again with a fine brush, add several shades of brown all over the face. Use light feathery strokes to give the impression of fur.

Add dots over the muzzle with the point of a fine brush.

Curve the line of the mouth upwards.

Monkey Business

White-Faced Monkey

1 Keeping your sponge fairly dry, apply a light brown or a beige base over the whole face.

2 Paint in the large white patch over the centre of the face.

3 Paint around the eyes in dark brown.

4 Apply a little light brown above and below the mouth, using a sponge or brush.

5 Paint the black nostrils and mouth. Add the fine lines around the mouth then, with a thick brush, add the black and white stripes.

IT'S AMAZING how easy it is to change the shape and appearance of someone's face with make-up. The eyes on these two faces look small and deepset because they have been outlined in dark colours. The baboon face looks long and pointed because we have lengthened the nose, taking the paint over the lips, and have used a bright colour to make it stand out. Both these faces will take practise and you'll need an older model who is prepared to sit still for you.

Don't paint too close to the eyes.

Baboon

1 Paint the nose and the heart-shaped area around the mouth in bright red.

2 Paint in black over the eyes and outline the sides of the red nose.

3 Paint in the dark blue area with a brush.

4 Paint in the dark brown above and below the eyes and on the cheeks.

5 Using a finer brush, paint lots of small feathery strokes over the rest of the face in dark brown, mid-brown and light brown.

6 Again with a fine brush, highlight the forehead in white and add the white highlights over the blue paint.

7 Paint in black over and around the mouth, then add the feathery white highlights over the top.

Brush paint into the hair and don't forget to paint the ears, too.

Red Parrot

1 Apply a thin peachy-coloured base over the whole face.

2 Paint the green ovals around the eyes then outline them in red.

3 Paint the red beak.

4 Outline the beak in black then paint the black patch over the red beak.

5 Paint in the red and blue feathers.

Use a fine brush to create the feathery design.

Lift the brush towards the end of each stroke for a softer look.

The black part of the beak should be narrower than the mouth.

Birds of Paradise

Peacock

First paint the peacock's pale blue body shape between the eyes and over the nose. Add the dark blue wings and crest, then paint in the white and black 'eyes' on the feathers. Add the yellow beak, outline it in black, paint the lips in blue and finish with a little glitter.

BIRDS MAKE GOOD FACE-PAINTING DESIGNS. From cute little budgies to exotic tropical parrots... Let your imagination soar! Again, you can make your designs quite simple to suit a younger child – just paint a wide yellow or red beak over the nose and mouth and brush some brightly coloured feathers around the edges of the face. The peacock mask is particularly good for older children and is a popular party face. Other birds can easily be painted as masks in the same way (see the butterfly masks on the next page).

Pink bird

1 Paint in the wide beak with a brush, outlining the shape in yellow first then filling it in with the same colour.

2 Paint in the black mouth, the laughter lines, and the lines by the nostrils and over the nose.

3 With a brush, paint bright pink, purple and white feathers over the forehead and on the chin.

▶ *Feather boas make perfect headdresses for tropical birds. Tie them in place under the chin or at the nape of the neck.*

Creepy Crawlies

Honeycomb

1 Apply a yellow base over the whole face with a sponge.

2 Paint the orange hexagons across the forehead and down the cheeks, then outline them in black.

3 Paint the yellow bodies of the bee and fly, then their white wings.

4 Outline the wings in black, paint in the heads then add the bee's stripes.

5 With a fine brush, add the black detail on the wings then highlight the honeycomb with a touch of white paint.

CREEPY CRAWLIES are always popular with children. If they have wings, they work well as a painted mask across the eyes. Otherwise, you can paint the whole creature as a small motif on the cheek. It's also fun to paint an insect crawling up your model's arm or leg. Remember that the smaller the motif, the fewer colours you should use so that the picture stands out clearly. If you paint a butterfly mask in bright, bold colours, you will not usually need to apply a base coat. Remember to make the pattern on your butterfly's wings symmetrical.

Bumblebee

A bee can be painted as a black mask over the eyes, with a bright yellow base. You could also paint a simple bee face by brushing yellow and black stripes horizontally across the face.

Always paint blocks of solid colour before outlining in black.

Use a thin brush to paint in the fine black veins.

Blue Butterfly

Paint the butterfly's pink body first, then paint the pale blue, pale green, orange and turquoise shapes above the eyes and over the cheeks. Paint in the black outline then the white antennae and the lines on the body.

Paint a large black spot on each lower wing.

Pink Butterfly

1 Apply a thin yellow base over the face with a fairly dry sponge.

2 Paint in the deep pink above the eyes first. Then, working from the top down, paint in each band of colour with a brush.

3 Outline each section in black with a fine brush then add the black dots.

4 Add the antennae and the detail down the nose.

5 Decorate with glitter gel, applying each colour of glitter with a clean, dry brush.

6 Paint the lips in deep blue and white.

Gold mesh makes a perfect party headdress. Wrap it around the head like a turban.

Party Motifs

Scorpion

1 Paint the shape of the scorpion on the cheek in orange then fill in with the same colour.

2 With a fine brush, outline the scorpion in black.

3 With the same brush, add the black detail on each section of the scorpion's body.

4 Add white highlights and paint in the eyes.

5 Outline the eyes with a fine brush and dot in their pupils.

SPIDERS AND SCORPIONS are popular motifs with teenagers – particularly at Hallowe'en. Webs take a bit of practice. Find a good photograph to work from and keep the lines as fine and delicate as you can.

Curve the lines on the web inwards.

Paint two thin black lines just under the eyes to make them stand out.

Spider

1 Sponge on a pale yellow base then, with the same sponge, add a little white over the forehead and down the nose. Here, we've used pearlised water-based make-up to give the skin a soft sheen.

2 Paint the spider's web in black using a fine brush.

3 Paint in the spider. Use two or three colours – here, black white with a touch of red.

4 Complete the effect with bright red lips and a little silver glitter to highlight the web.

Something Fishy

TROPICAL FISH and other sea creatures are wonderful for face painting because of their bright, exotic colours and patterns. Look in books to get more ideas – jellyfish, sharks, beautiful shells and angel fish would all make fantastic face-painting designs. Here are some tiger fish and leaping dolphins to start you off. Omit a base coat or sponge blue water-based make-up over the whole face or just one cheek, as shown below.

Tiger Fish

1 Paint the fish shapes in orange with a brush then fill in with the same colour.

2 Outline both fish in black then add their black stripes and eyes.

3 Paint on the white stripes with the edge of a wide brush (see more on this technique on page 15).

4 Paint in the white bubbles with the tip of a brush.

5 Paint on the seaweed in green and white.

Flamingo and Crab

Sponge some pale blue over part of each face. Mark out your shapes first in pink or orange then fill them in with the same colour. Again, we've added touches of glitter gel to the designs for a party look.

Brush a little white over the dolphins' backs and tails, to highlight.

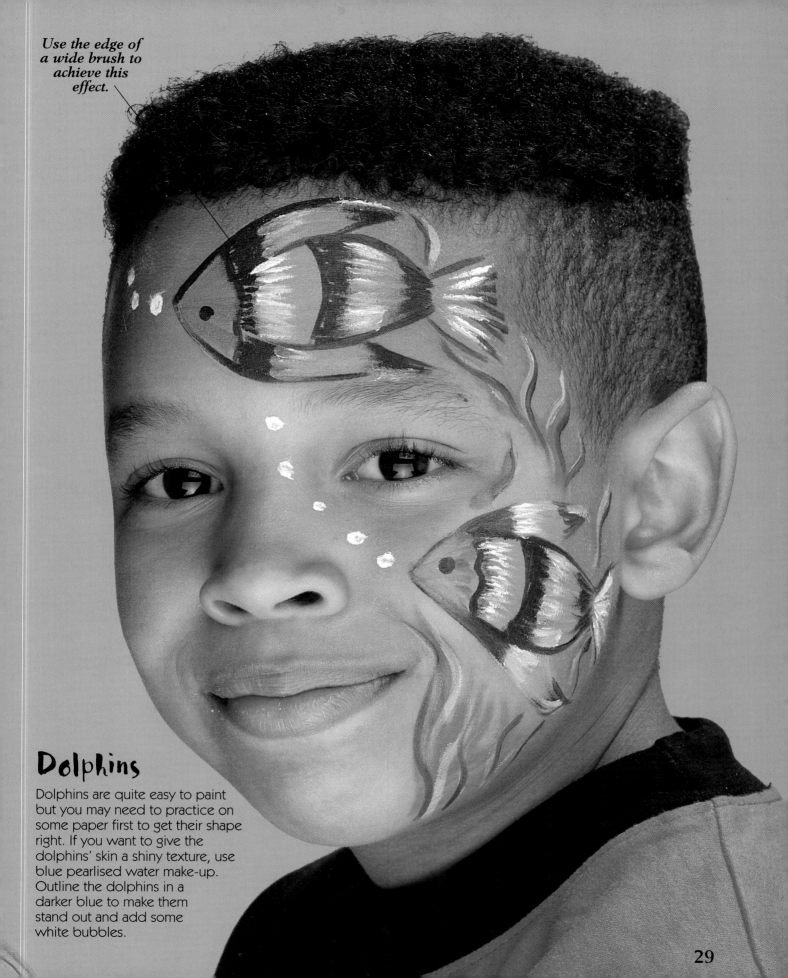

Use the edge of a wide brush to achieve this effect.

Dolphins

Dolphins are quite easy to paint but you may need to practice on some paper first to get their shape right. If you want to give the dolphins' skin a shiny texture, use blue pearlised water make-up. Outline the dolphins in a darker blue to make them stand out and add some white bubbles.

Going Green

Green Frog

1 Sponge a thin yellow base over the whole face.

2 Paint around the outside of the face in green with a thick brush. Use a darker green to paint the chin.

3 Paint in the white areas above the eyes then outline them in brown.

4 Paint the lips in brown, extending the lines on either side to make a wide frog's mouth.

5 Paint dark blue lines over the forehead and on either side of the mouth.

GREEN SCALEY OR SLIMY CREATURES are always popular faces. The special pearlised make-up we used for the spider on page 27 and the dolphins on page 29 works particularly well if you want to paint shiny reptile skin. We've used it for the dinosaur face on the right, but have painted the green frog in ordinary water-based face paint.

Sponge a little green paint into your model's hair. It will wash out easily with ordinary shampoo.

Terrible Lizard

1 Apply a pearlised light green base with a damp sponge.

2 Using the same sponge, apply a darker shade of pearlised green around the outer edges of the face. Again with the same sponge, blend a little red over the cheeks and just under the eyes.

3 With a brush, paint in the shapes above the eyes and over the nose. Use a large brush to blend the green paint inwards. You will need to do this before the green outline dries, so work quickly and apply the paint a little at a time.

4 Paint in the green mouth, just over the model's chin.

5 Paint the lips in white, add the white teeth, then outline the teeth in black with a fine brush.

6 Paint in the black nostrils over your model's upper lip.

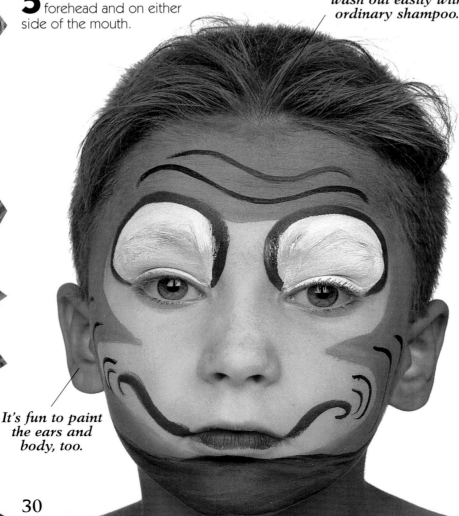

It's fun to paint the ears and body, too.

A green wig bought from a costume shop completes the effect.

Gallery

Bryony Holiman

THE PUBLISHERS would like to thank all the models – who look very different without their make-up – and face painters Lauren Staton and Wilhelmina Barnden.

Many thanks also to George Jackson (Patch and Leaping Lamb), Victoria Sloman (Party Mouse and Crab), Eleanor Yeandle (Pink Rabbit), Louise Ahearn (Cheeky Mouse), Charles Bullock (Frog and Panda), Josephine Aldridge (Baboon, Blue Cat and Spider), and Kelly Randall (Zebra).

Amy Nicholls
(and Pink Cat)

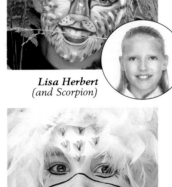

Lisa Herbert
(and Scorpion)

Katy Nicholls

Emma Ryan
(and Brown Bear and Terrible Lizard)

James Bullock

Kate Gibbs

Amy Wigglesworth

Andrea Stradling

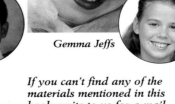

Luke Ngakane

Gemma Jeffs

Jonathan Aldridge
(and Cockerel, Sheep and Honeycomb)

◤ KINGFISHER
First published 1997 by Kingfisher
This edition published 2012 by Kingfisher
an imprint of Macmillan Children's Books
20 New Wharf Road, London N1 9RR
Associated companies throughout the world
www.panmacmillan.com
ISBN 978-0-7534-3464-2
Copyright © In-Resort Services Ltd 1997
All rights reserved. Printed in China
A CIP catalogue record for this book
is available from the British Library.
9 8 7 6 5 4 3 2 1
1TR/0112/WKT/UTD(PICA)/140MA

If you can't find any of the materials mentioned in this book, write to us for a mail order catalogue at:

Snazaroo,
Unit 1A-1D Brunel Way,
Mart Road Industrial Estate,
Minehead,
Somerset TA24 5BJ,
United Kingdom.

Hannah Ngakane
(and Blue Butterfly)